Bird Nests

THERESE HOPKINS

PowerKiDS press.
New York

Published in 2009 by The Rosen Publishing Group, Inc.
29 East 21st Street, New York, NY 10010

Copyright © 2009 by The Rosen Publishing Group, Inc.

First Edition

Editor: Nicole Pristash
Book Design: Kate Laczynski
Photo Researcher: Jessica Gerweck

Photo Credits: Cover, pp. 1, 5, 7, 9, 11, 13, 19, 23, 24 Shutterstock.com; p. 15 © Ralph Lee Hopkins/Getty Images, Inc.; p. 17 © Laure Neish/www.istockphoto.com; p. 21 © Nico Limmen/www.istockphoto.com; p. 24 (hatch) © Gina Hanf/www.istockphoto.com.

Library of Congress Cataloging-in-Publication Data

Hopkins, Therese.
  Bird nests / Therese Hopkins.— 1st ed.
     p. cm. — (Home sweet home)
  Includes index.
  ISBN-13: 978-1-4358-2693-9 (library binding) — ISBN 978-1-4358-3067-7 (pbk.)
ISBN 978-1-4358-3079-0 (6-pack)
  1. Birds—Nests—Juvenile literature. I. Title.
  QL675.H78 2009
  598.156'4—dc22

                                            2008019533

Manufactured in the United States of America

CONTENTS

A bird nest is a place where a mother bird lays her eggs.

Bird nests can also keep baby birds safe after they **hatch**.

To build their nests, many birds use small sticks and grass that the birds gather from the ground.

9

This woodpecker is making its nest by digging a hole in a tree with its **beak**.

11

Robins build nests in between tree **branches** to keep their nests safe.

13

Some birds build nests that hang down from tree branches.

This bluebird has made its nest inside a hole in a tree.

Flamingos lay their eggs on **mounds** of mud.

Ducks use grass and sticks to make nests on the ground.

Birds take good care of their nests by adding more leaves and grass to the nests.

23

beak

branches

hatch

mounds

WEB SITES

Due to the changing nature of Internet links, PowerKids Press has developed an online list of Web sites related to the subject of this book. This site is updated regularly. Please use this link to access the list:
www.powerkidslinks.com/hsh/bnests/